BABY STEPS TO MEDITATION

A Step by Step Guide to Meditation

Gudjon Bergmann

www.babystepstomeditation.com

The program presented in this little book is based on 20 years of teaching and studying meditation. It represents a simplified version of what ancient meditative traditions and current scientific researchers agree on.

To inquire about workshops, book a private lesson or to get more information please visit
www.babystepstomeditation.com

Baby Steps to Meditation

Copyright © 2014 by Gudjon Bergmann

All rights reserved. No part of this book may be reproduced or transmitted in any form or by any means without written permission of the author.

TABLE OF CONTENTS

WHY TAKE BABY STEPS? 1

   THE BUILDING BLOCKS 2

STEP 1 UNDERSTANDING & MOTIVATION 5

   UNDERSTANDING 6

   MOTIVATION 9

   YOUR STICK 14

   YOUR CARROT 15

STEP 2 PREPARING THE BODY WITH RELAXATION 17

   THE RELAXATION POSE 18

   RELAXATION TECHNIQUES 20

   TENSE AND RELAX 20

- DEEP BREATHING 22
- BELLY PUMP 23
- MENTAL RELAXATION 24
- MEASUREMENTS 25
- MUSIC OR NO MUSIC? 27
- PRACTICE & PERSONALIZATION 28

STEP 3 PREPARING THE MIND WITH CONCENTRATION 29

- THE ALERTNESS POSE 31
- FOCUS ON A WORD OR PHRASE 33
- ALERT AWARENESS 36
- MEASUREMENTS 37
- PERSONALIZATION & PRACTICE 39

STEP 4 UNCOVERING THE MEDITATIVE STATE 41

- PRACTICE & PERSONALIZATION 45

ENJOY EACH STEP.. 47

STAY IN TOUCH 51

WHY TAKE BABY STEPS?

Consider the following.

When you learned how to read, you first learned the letters, then how to combine them into words, and finally you learned to form sentences… and you became better with practice, practice, practice.

Learning meditation is much the same.

If you have a good golf teacher, he will teach you one thing and tell you to work on it. Then you go home and practice. Next time he will teach you another thing. You go home and practice… and so on, each lesson layering, building on the previous lessons and the practice that you have done on your own.

Learning meditation is much the same.

Many piano teachers will send their pupils home if they perceive at the beginning of a lesson that the student has not practiced at home. They understand the importance of practice. Without practice, piano playing is only theory.

Again, learning meditation is much the same.

There is learning. There is practice. There is more learning. Then more practice. You keep on going until you achieve the meditative state.

There are *no short cuts*.

THE BUILDING BLOCKS

The building blocks of meditation are relaxation and concentration. If you cannot relax, you cannot meditate. If you cannot concentrate, you cannot meditate. No exceptions.

In this short book you will learn how to achieve the meditative state, starting with understanding and motivation (ABC's), then relaxation (words), moving on to concentration (sentences), and finally to the meditative state (fully literate).

If you follow the program and practice, practice, practice, you will learn the art of meditation.

And you will understand meditation.

In the future you will learn more about meditative states and nuances of the mind, but even so, the basic practices you learn in this book will last you for a lifetime.

Meditation will be a part of you…

…if you take baby steps…

…one step at a time.

STEP 1
UNDERSTANDING
& MOTIVATION

Step one in this program is mental preparation — providing both understanding and motivation.

You need *understanding* to become self-reliant. Understanding will allow you to think clearly and ask the right questions when faced with conflicting information.

You need *motivation* because achieving the meditative state takes practice. You must act in order to experience the meditative state. Personalized motivation will encourage you to practice regularly with persistence.

UNDERSTANDING

The terms relaxation, concentration and meditation are thrown around in our society, often meaning different things to different people.

Let us begin by making sure we are on the same page. The following definitions will help you better understand each of these important terms as you embark on your journey.

Relaxation is… a state between waking and sleeping, where the body is completely still and the mind is allowed to flow freely from one thought to another, or alternately, a state in which the mind becomes inadvertently calm.

It is a rejuvenating and energizing state. Where laziness drains energy, relaxation provides energy. You don't have to empty the mind. Simply calm the body.

Concentration is… a relaxed mental state, where the stream of consciousness flows in a single direction, either focusing on a phrase or mental picture, or alternately, a state in which the mind is alert and aware.

Step 1 – Understanding & Motivation

You don't have to strain to concentrate. For the purposes of meditation, concentration should be relaxed.

Meditation is… a state that can best be described as deep dreamless sleep while awake.

In the meditative state, mental activity is reduced to a point where the mind feels empty, but it is not. The mind waves are simply working at an extremely low rate.

Therefore, used in this context, meditation is not a verb. It is not something you "do". It is a state you enter into.

This is the great *conundrum*.

Think of it this way. You can consciously raise your right hand. You can consciously close your eyes. But, you cannot consciously fall asleep, right at this moment.

You can prepare for sleep. But, sleep is not something you "do". It is a state change. You transition from one state to another.

The practices that precede sleep are (1) lying down and (2) closing your eyes. You don't "do" sleep. You lie down and close your eyes. Then sleep comes.

In the same way, the practices that precede meditation are (1) relaxation and (2) concentration. You don't "do" meditation. You sit still, relax, and concentrate. Then the meditative state comes.

You can practice relaxation, because you can consciously withdraw tension from different parts of your body. You can practice concentration, because you can consciously focus your mind. But, as stated before, and contrary to popular belief, you cannot practice meditation.

That is because meditation is a state, similar to sleep (often referred to as the fourth state — as in (1) waking, (2) dreaming, (3) dreamless sleep, and (4) meditation).

The transition from waking to sleeping is similar to the transition from waking to the meditative state.

When people use the term meditation like a verb (i.e. "to meditate"), they are usual-

Step 1 — Understanding & Motivation

ly referring to the practices that precede the state of meditation.

While it is quite alright to use the phrase "to meditate", you need to understand that you are in most cases referring to the *practices*, not the *state*.

This is the understanding that you need to proceed. First, that the practice of meditation is really the practice of relaxation and concentration, and second, that meditation is not something that you "do", but rather a state that you enter into when you have created the right circumstances.

MOTIVATION

Human beings are driven by purpose. They will not do anything unless they see *why* it can be helpful, either to them or someone they care for.

You are a human being.

If you want to learn how to reach the meditative state, you must understand why the practice will be beneficial to you.

Motivation is the key. If you are not motivated, you will not practice. You will see no point in practicing.

On the other hand, if you are motivated, you will practice and reap the rewards.

People are generally motivated by pleasure, pain, or a combination of the two. That is why you need to answer the following questions:

1) What will a regular meditation practice help me *reduce* or get rid of?
2) What will a regular meditation practice help me *increase* or acquire?

Pain is a better motivator. Start with that. What kind of discomfort can meditation help you decrease?

Stress, anxiety, depression, and physical tension are at the top of that list. Even a small reduction can be tremendously beneficial.

While meditation will not eradicate any of the above, it has been shown to reduce the symptoms quite effectively.

Step 1 — Understanding & Motivation

Suffer from insomnia? Research has shown that people who meditate fall asleep faster and sleep better.

Struggle with addiction? A regular meditation practice has been used to supplement addiction treatments with good results.

What about the positive aspects? What can meditation help you increase or acquire?

Increased concentration, creativity and overall energy are at the top of that list — all valuable traits in our society.

But the main acquisition, so to speak, is that with the practice of meditation you can reach an inner state of peace at will — a state of equilibrium.

You can create your *moments of peace*.

You see, meditation is not a fabricated state. It is natural. It is accessible to all. And in the same way that a person who learns how to run, can run any time they want to, or, a person who knows how to play an instrument can play music at will, once you learn how to meditate, you can create your moments of peace at will.

This ability, to access a peaceful state of mind, at will, should suffice as motivation — but it doesn't. Human beings need personal reasons to motivate them to action.

- *"Should I watch TV or practice?"*
- *"Should I grab a beer or practice?"*
- *"Should I go online or practice?"*

Those are some of the questions you will be faced with when you start to practice meditation. That is why mental preparation is extremely important.

Imagine…

… feeling less stress. How will that positively affect your relationship with your friends and family? How will it reduce mental and physical tension?

… sleeping better. Can you see how better quality of sleep will give you energy that lasts throughout the day?

Step 1 — Understanding & Motivation

… being less prone to depression and anxiety. Meditation has certainly been shown to help in that department.

… being more focused and creative. How will you work and play more productively?

The key, the secret, the most important aspect, is that you must make your own list. It must be detailed.

It must be *personal*.

Once you experience the benefits of meditation firsthand, then your list can evolve and change, but by then your meditation practice will likely feed off itself. You will need less of a stick, because the practice will be the carrot.

Answer the following questions. Think about yourself, your family, your friends, your work, and your hobbies.

Write. Take your time. Lay the foundation for your practice.

YOUR STICK

Imagine and answer: "What will a regular meditation practice help me *reduce* or get rid of?"

_____

_____

_____

_____

_____

_____

_____

_____

_____

_____

Step 1 — Understanding & Motivation

YOUR CARROT

Imagine and answer: "What will a regular meditation practice help me *increase* or acquire?"

_____

_____

_____

_____

_____

_____

_____

_____

_____

_____

STEP 2
PREPARING THE BODY WITH RELAXATION

A relaxed body enables the mind to become focused. If the body is stiff, tense, agitated, and restless, then meditation is all but impossible. It is necessary to prepare the body and learn how to relax before moving on to mental exercises.

Step two focuses on several relaxation techniques and teaches you how to personalize your relaxation practice.

For simplification, relaxation techniques can be split into two categories.

- Physical
- Mental

Because the mental practices are also related to concentration, which is the next step, you will primarily learn physical practices in this part of the process and only be introduced to the simplest mental practice.

Your *goal* is to reach a state where the body is completely still and relaxed, and stay in that state for ten to fifteen minutes at least once before proceeding to the next step.

Achieving this may take anywhere from a couple of attempts to a couple of months, depending on your current state of physical tension.

THE RELAXATION POSE

One of the main differences between relaxation and meditation is the state of alertness required for meditation, which is not required for relaxation. Therefore, lying down is preferable when relaxing, while sitting is imperative when practicing meditation. For maximum benefits, use the following guidelines when preparing the body for relaxation.

Step 2 — Relaxation

Lie on your back on a semi-hard surface. If the surface is too soft or too hard, it may increase tension.

For comfort you may place a small pillow under your head and/or roll a blanket under your knees for lower back support (both are optional).

Keep your spine fairly straight and head centered. Allow your feet to be apart and point your toes away from the body (this will relax the legs and the hips).

Your hands point slightly away from your body (never above the shoulders, as this will cut off circulation) and your palms are facing up (this is comfortable for ninety percent of people, whereas some find it more comfortable to have the palms facing towards the body, or, in a few cases, facing down).

Once you are lying still you may want to gently move your shoulder blades (apart or together) and hips (up or down) into a more comfortable position.

Use this posture to practice the following relaxation techniques.

Note that if your body is very tense or restless it can be beneficial to do physical exercises, such as walking or stretching, prior to attempting to relax.

RELAXATION TECHNIQUES

Try each of the following techniques as a standalone practice first—then you can experiment with combinations.

For beginners, shorter and more frequent practices are better. Start with five to ten minutes, all the way down to two minutes if that is all you can cope with when you begin. At the early stages, regularity is more important than length of time. Slowly work your way up to the goal of being completely relaxed for ten to fifteen minutes.

TENSE AND RELAX

Engaging the body is the simplest form of relaxation. It also helps beginners feel like they are "doing" something.

Tensing the muscles combines surface tension with deeper muscle tension, so

Step 2 — Relaxation

that when you release, you release both the conscious tension you created and the underlying tension that was already there.

You can either (1) tense all the muscles of the body at the same time and then relax completely, or (2) tense one body part at a time and relax.

Tensing all the muscles is faster, but tensing one muscle group at a time brings on a deeper state of relaxation. Combine the tensing and relaxing with your breathing by inhaling when you tense and exhaling when you relax.

If you plan to tense the entire body at the same time, you can repeat the exercise two to three times for maximum effects.

If you plan to tense one muscle group at a time, try this sequence.

- Right leg
- Left leg
- Buttocks
- Abdomen
(inhale and expand the belly)
- Chest
(inhale and expand the chest)

- Arms
  (raise them slightly and make fists, then spread the fingers)
- Face

Experiment with how long you hold the tension in each muscle group (or the entire body at the same time). Remember to inhale when you tense and exhale when you release.

DEEP BREATHING

Using breathing techniques can allow you to relax anywhere and anytime, but when combined with the relaxation pose, deep breathing can be an extremely helpful tool.

First, you need to understand that deep breathing is not breathing into your belly, but rather deeper into your lungs, thusly pushing the diaphragm down and expanding your belly.

(Air in your belly causes belching, while air deep in your lungs is nourishing and calming.)

Step 2 — Relaxation

When you inhale, expand your belly as much as you can and then expand your chest area, all the while keeping the shoulders relaxed.

When you exhale, relax your chest and belly, and try to empty your lungs completely.

Repeat this at least ten times.

If you feel lightheaded, return your breathing back to normal.

At first your breathing may feel tense and uncomfortable. You may be tempted to breathe loudly with vigor. Resist that urge. For calming effects, deep breathing should become slow and rhythmic. That is why you practice deep breathing — to slow down. Consciously try to breathe as deep and as slowly as you can, while making as little noise as you can.

BELLY PUMP

A combination of deep breathing and tensing, this technique works quickly to reduce tension.

First, assume the relaxation pose.

Then, inhale and fill your lungs.

Hold your breath and pump your belly up (belly button pushed towards the ceiling) and down (belly button pulled towards the spine) as often as you can without letting the air out.

When you can no longer hold the air in, exhale and relax completely. Repeat once or twice for maximum effects.

MENTAL RELAXATION

This is similar to the tense and relax exercise, but instead of doing anything physically, you scan your body mentally for tension, and mentally relax one body part at a time.

Depending on the time you have, you can focus on large parts of the body, which takes less time, or focus on smaller body parts, which takes more time.

Step 2 — Relaxation

For larger parts you consciously relax your legs, then your hips, your back and so on.

For smaller parts you consciously relax your toes, then soles of your feet, tops of your feet, ankles, shins, calves and so on.

Remember, that although this is a semi-concentration exercise, the goal is physical relaxation, so even if your mind wanders after mentally relaxing a few body parts, you have nonetheless achieved your goal if you reach a relaxed state. If however, the body does not relax, refocus on consciously relaxing one body part at a time.

MEASUREMENTS

Relaxation is a state in between waking and sleeping. Therefore you can have several different experiences when relaxing, all of them beneficial. But, you need to know when you are relaxing and when you are not.

Here are some measurements to help you.

First, your body needs to be *mostly still*. That is the important measurement. Yes, mostly still, because sometimes there are inadvertent and slight movements of the fingers, toes and eyes when the body is ridding itself of tension. However, if you start consciously moving body parts in the relaxation pose, then that is a sign that you are not relaxing.

Second, allow your *mind to flow freely*. If your mind becomes obsessed with one thought or idea, then you are not relaxing. If it is mostly inactive, then you are relaxing, and if your mind flows from one thought or idea to another, like when you are dreaming, you are still relaxing.

You neither need to put a leash on your mind, nor do you have to empty your mind in order to relax.

Third, you *feel better afterwards* than you did before. With practice, relaxation should increase energy and you should feel better. The exception is that when you begin to relax regularly you may feel more tired afterwards. If that happens, then that is your body asking for more rest. Keep relaxing and you will not only overcome that feeling, but also gain energy and a feeling of wellbeing.

MUSIC OR NO MUSIC?

All the techniques taught in this program can be used without music or other types of accompaniment such as special mats, blankets, meditation beads, etc. All you need is your body, your mind, and a quiet place.

However, quiet places are increasingly hard to come by almost anywhere in the world. When you can't find a quiet place, using music or nature sounds to drown out ambient noises is a good practice.

If you prefer music to nature sounds then the soundtrack you choose should be instrumental and as neutral as possible. Yes, you can like the music, but make sure that it doesn't rile up any emotions, neither good nor bad. You want the music to be in the background and let the relaxation take center stage. This is also true when choosing music for concentration practices and meditation.

PRACTICE & PERSONALIZATION

First, try each of the techniques on their own — at least two or three times. Get a first-hand experience of how each of them makes you feel. Take notes.

Second, combine two, three, or even all of the techniques into one practice, based on your preferences.

Third, set up a practice schedule. Your primary goal is to create a habit, so regularity is more important than the length of time to begin with. Practice anywhere from 3 to 6 times a week.

Fourth, practice until you reach a relaxed state easily and can stay in that state for at least 10 to 15 minutes continuously.

STEP 3
PREPARING THE MIND WITH CONCENTRATION

Any type of concentrated mental activity or directed stream of consciousness falls into the category of concentration.

Whether one is remaining alert (mindfulness), focusing on a single thought or phrase (mantra), or mentally exploring ones inner world (visualization), all are one form of concentration or another.

To refresh your memory, meditation can be defined as "deep dreamless sleep awake", so concentrated mental activity is *not* meditation, although mental activities like visualization are quite often mislabeled as meditation in our society. Once you understand this, you have an easier time navigating the misleading variety of so called "meditation techniques" that are out there.

(This means that any type of visualization, such as guided imagery or focusing on colors, is not meditation as we have defined it. Therefore you will not learn any visualization techniques in this book. Visualization has other benefits, such as elevating emotional states from negative to positive, physical healing, activating the imagination/intuition, and uncovering the shadow aspects of the psyche, all valuable, although visualization rarely leads to the meditative state.)

Concentration *is the doorway* through which the meditative state becomes available. The two concentration exercises that are most likely to bring about the meditative state are (1) focusing on a word or phrase (mantra) and (2) alert awareness, which is a form of relaxed concentration (mindfulness).

In step three you will learn both types of mental training.

Step 3 — Concentration

The difference between the two can be explained thusly. If you were looking at a *Where is Waldo?* picture, then concentration would mean looking for Waldo and then staying focused on Waldo when you find him, while alert awareness would mean allowing your mind to focus on the entire picture and if your mind latches onto specifics then you would practice letting go and again focusing on the entire picture.

THE ALERTNESS POSE

For the nervous system to stay awake and alert, both during concentration and meditation, *your spine needs to be erect*. That is the most important aspect of the meditation pose. Everything else is minor in comparison.

If you sit on a chair, you can either sit against the back (if straight) or sit at the front of the seat with your spine erect.

If you sit cross legged on the floor (not necessary, but beneficial for those who can), keep a small pillow under your tailbone to keep your spine erect with a slight arch in the lower back (the same method can be used when you sit on a chair, a pillow can support the natural arch of your lower back).

You should not begin focusing your mind until your body is still. Getting to that point can include gentle stretching, breathing and repositioning for a couple of minutes.

Once your spine is erect and your body is still, try to relax. Use what you have learned in the previous step (relaxation). Relax your arms in your lap or on your knees. Relax your shoulders. Relax your torso as much as you can without slumping, without your head rolling forward, backward or sideways. Relax your legs and keep your spine erect.

Once you feel relaxed and awake (spine erect) at the same time, then you have entered the pose.

The alertness pose may take some time to master. Sometimes, all you will be able to do for the entire session is adjust your body until it is comfortable — over and over again. That is a valuable practice in itself. The body needs training in order to stay still, same as the mind.

FOCUS ON A WORD OR PHRASE

Focusing on a word or phrase is the most common concentration method and has been taught throughout history as a meditation practice, often with religious connotations.

Modern research has found that any word or phrase will do. However, some research suggests that people who use a word or phrase that has personal meaning to them are more likely to continue with their meditation practice, which means that personalizing is part of creating motivation.

By focusing on a word or phrase, the mind slows down and gradually drowns out continuous mental chatter.

The emphasis is on *gradually*.

A big part of using this method is being OK with the fact that the mind will wander. Wandering is the nature of the mind.

In the same way that a weightlifter gets stronger by lifting weights, the mind gets stronger when you gradually tame it´s wandering nature. The wandering mind is not disturbing the practice (as many novices think when they begin). Gently struggling with the mind *is the practice*.

Before you begin to practice you need to choose a word or phrase. Single words like Love, Light, Calm, Peace, and Relax, are all good examples of effective focus words.

Religions, such as Hinduism and Buddhism, both have a strong meditative foundation and offer a variety of words and phrases (mantras) from which to choose from.

People with a Christian background may want to choose phrases like "Thy Will Be Done" or *Maranatha* (Aramaic for "Come Lord").

Step 3 — Concentration

Atheists and agnostics can choose any word or phrase that speaks to their peaceful mental side.

The goal is to find a word or phrase that you resonate with personally, because you will be repeating the word or phrase mentally on a continual basis for years to come if you stick with the practice.

Once you have chosen a word and are ready to begin, it is time to sit in the concentration and meditation pose and relax.

When your body is still and relaxed, focus on repeating the word or phrase in your mind, either continuously, or in rhythm with your breathing (i.e. inhale and say your chosen word/phrase in your mind, exhale and say your chosen word/phrase in your mind).

When your mind wanders, gently bring your attention back to the word or phrase, without any judgment.

To summarize, you sit, you relax, you focus, and you gently bring your mind back to the word or phrase when your mind wanders.

Begin with 5 minutes of concentration, and then work your way up to 10 to 20 minutes with time.

ALERT AWARENESS

Imagine sitting on the porch of a coffee house in a busy city, being relaxed and taking in the entire scenery — the entire picture. You are a passive observer, not involved in anything that is going on.

That is alert awareness (mindfulness) in a nutshell.

But instead of keeping your eyes open, you close your eyes and passively observe your mind, non-judgmentally and without getting caught up in any one thought.

The key to alert awareness is letting go and not allowing any one thought or image to dominate your mind for an extended period of time. Whether the thought is pleasurable or painful, it doesn't matter, simply let it go and allow

Step 3 — Concentration

your mind to be alert to the entirety of what you experience (both through the senses and in the mind).

Gradually, your mind will calm down.

Using this method, your focus is on letting go and passively *observing*. That is the concentration part of the practice.

Although very different from the previous concentration exercise, the effects are similar.

(However, note that your ability to concentrate is not trained to the same level of proficiency when you use the alert awareness technique.)

In the same manner as before, you start with 5 minutes and gradually work your way up to 10 to 20 minutes.

MEASUREMENTS

Your mind is much harder to tame than your body. Remember that and go easy on yourself. In the monastic traditions of every major religion, novices often underwent years of concentration training before they were allowed to move on to the next phase of their meditative training.

While that may not be the case for you, it is important to practice with vigilance and vigor, while at the same time being easy on yourself when it comes to perceived achievements.

Progress is measured inch by inch.

Also, remember that your mental state can change from day to day, and your ability to focus may depend on a variety of factors, including your mental chatter, your physical state, and external events (over which you have no control). The following are a couple of ways to measure progress, depending on which method of concentration you use.

Word or phrase

When your mind settles down with more ease and you spend more time focusing on your chosen word or phrase and less time recovering from distractions, then you are making progress.

Step 3 — Concentration

Alert awareness

When you spend more time on passive observation and less time on getting caught up in your own thoughts, images and feelings (physical and emotional), then you are making progress.

PERSONALIZATION & PRACTICE

First, try each concentration practice for a week (at least five times per week) for a minimum of 5-10 minutes per session. Journal about your experiences.

Second, choose either practice to continue with on your own, or, combine practices (for example, starting with a word or phrase, and then retreating to alert awareness half way through your practice).

Third, continue with your chosen practice and learn how to discern the meditative state (next step).

STEP 4 UNCOVERING THE MEDITATIVE STATE

As previously stated, meditation is not something that you "do". It is a state you transition into when the circumstances are right.

With the practice of the relaxation and concentration techniques in this program you create the right circumstances.

In step four you are ready to *discern* the meditative state, so that you can recognize it and enjoy it when it comes.

This is where many people get confused. They think that the practices explained thus far in the program are "meditation", because they confuse practices with the state of being, which is called meditation.

Let's revisit the definition.

"Meditation can be likened to deep dreamless sleep awake."

That is how you discern — by contemplating the definition.

When you are practicing relaxation and concentration techniques and your mind becomes *completely still* — even for a brief period of time — that is meditation.

Do not treat these moments of stillness like a distraction from the practice of focusing the mind. Enjoy those moments and they will become longer.

These *moments of stillness* are meditation.

The concentration and relaxation practices are only the tools.

Once you have used the ladder (relaxation and concentration) to reach the top (meditation), then you should enjoy the

Step 4 — Meditation

scenery, instead of getting right back on the ladder.

"Deep dreamless sleep awake."

That is meditation.

One more time for clarification.

The moments of peace *in between* the mental practices *are meditation*.

Other words that describe the state are…

…peaceful
…blissful
…vast
…calm
…clear

But, all words and descriptions fall short. The meditative experience is beyond words. That is why reading this book is not enough. Learning from a teacher is not enough. Only practice will produce experience. And experience will produce *first hand* understanding.

Imagine a time before you had ever had chocolate. Going to lectures about chocolate would have been interesting. Reading about chocolate might have increased your appetite. But only tasting chocolate would have really made you understand how good chocolate can be. Only tasting— only experience.

There is an old saying about how we should look where the master is pointing, not at the finger of the master.

The finger is the practice, where he is pointing is the state of meditation. Don't mistake the finger for the destination. Don't mistake the practice for the state.

In steps two and three you learned how to prepare for meditation. Now, in step four, you are learning how to discern when you are experiencing the meditative state.

To begin with, the meditative state may come for a few moments at a time. With practice, you will enter the state more often and for longer periods of time.

Step 4 — Meditation

PRACTICE & PERSONALIZATION

At this point, if you have followed the steps, you should already have a concentration practice going.

All you do now is add increased *awareness*, noticing when you *enter* the meditative state (the mind becomes still) and when you *exit* the meditative state (the mind becomes active — this includes enjoyable mental activities such as positive emotional experiences and colorful visualizations). When the mind becomes active you return to your practice (focus on a word or phrase or maintain alert awareness).

The key is to enjoy it when your mind is in a state of peace, because the moments of peace are effectively the meditative state.

ENJOY EACH STEP

It is human nature to be impatient. We all want results and we want them fast. But, when practicing meditation, impatience is a hindrance.

So, instead of waiting for the meditative state and being frustrated every time you don't achieve it, learn to enjoy all the benefits that come with each progressive step.

Enjoy the benefits of physical relaxation. Even if you do nothing else, a regular relaxation practice can do wonders.

Be happy when you can sit still for a few minutes. Taming the body to be still is an important step.

Even if you sit still and keep thinking about all the things that are going on in your life, be happy about that as well.

Baby Steps to Meditation

Although you are not in the state of meditation, the act of stepping back and thinking clearly about your life can be extremely helpful. You can solve many of your problems that way.

All the steps are beneficial in one way or another.

However, it may be helpful to point out that practicing meditation can be like taking two steps forward and then taking one step back.

You may experience days, when your mind become still with little or no effort. Then, you may experience days when you find no solace in any of the practices.

Feel free to revisit any of the steps at any time.

- If your practice is derailed, revisit step one (motivation).
- If your body is too agitated or stiff for sitting, revisit step two (relaxation). Sometimes lying down and relaxing can be more beneficial than sitting and trying to stay with the concentration exercises when

Enjoy Each Step

> your body is tired and your mind restless.
- Keep using the practices from step three (concentration), because they are most likely to create the right conditions for the meditative state.

These steps are simple. They should be simple. Simplicity is everywhere in nature, and meditation is a natural state. Meditation is a state of peaceful equilibrium, the fourth state of consciousness, and is always available to every single human being.

Even if you feel like nothing is happening, stick to the practices. Build a foundation by working on each step. Keep knocking on the door and you will get an answer.

You will experience *your moments of peace*.

STAY IN TOUCH

Thank you for reading the book. Hopefully the directions have been helpful.

If you would like additional information or personal feedback, please visit the website:

www.babystepstomeditation.com

On the website you will find information about private sessions and upcoming workshops.

When you sign up for the newsletter you will receive an instant **coupon** towards one of our workshops.

If you have any questions or comment, please contact the author by sending an e-mail to *gbergmann@gbergmann.com*.

Made in the USA
Charleston, SC
16 August 2014